A
Panorama of the
Holy Land

British Library Cataloguing in Publication Data. A catalogue record for this book is available from the British Library.

Published by Eagle, an imprint of Inter Publishing Service (IPS) Ltd, St Nicholas House, 14 The Mount, Guildford, Surrey GU2 5HN.

Typeset by Eagle Publishing
Printed in Singapore
ISBN No: 0 86347 171 4

A
Panorama of the Holy Land

Text by Stephen Sizer
Photographs by Jon Arnold

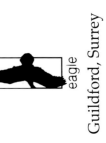

eagle

Guildford, Surrey

Contents

JEZREEL PLAIN, ISRAEL

Preface

MASADA, NEAR DEAD SEA, JORDAN RIFT VALLEY, ISRAEL

A book like this is precious both for what it can give and because it whets our appetites for more: if you have seen the country then it will revive your memories and recollections; if you have not, it may inspire you with eagerness to do so.

This is a book to savour. Each page introduces you to another place steeped in biblical history and abiding relevance. This is indeed the birthplace of our faith in the Lord Jesus Christ.

But there is much more to see in the Holy Land than ancient archaeological sites. There is here a vibrant but ancient church that has been here witnessing faithfully to Christ since the first Pentecost. If and when you do come, make it a priority to meet with us, the local Christians of your mother Church. Take time to visit a school or hospital run by one of the churches in Israel and Palestine. Our very future here is at stake.

May I extend to you a heartfelt welcome on behalf of your brothers and sisters in Christ – come and visit the land these moving photographs portray, and have fellowship with us. Then we shall both be enriched and blessed.

I pray that this book will enrich your sympathies and deepen your knowledge of the events which have made Palestine a Holy Land and Jerusalem the joy of the whole earth, a synonym of the City of God.

Riah Abu El-Assal, Bishop of Jerusalem

Introduction

OLIVE GROVE, ISRAEL

Palestine, Israel, the Promised Land, the Holy Land; the very name we use says as much about us and our presuppositions and aspirations as about this inscrutable, hypnotic, exotic location. Historically the birthplace of the Judeo-Christian heritage, it is today claimed by two peoples, the Jews and the Palestinians, its holy sites shared, at times uneasily, by three religions, Jewish, Christian and Moslem, often in close proximity as at the Temple Mount in Jerusalem or the tomb of Rachel in Bethlehem. Baraba Tuchman summarises some of the reasons why this place holds such fascination to so many.

More blood has been shed for Palestine than for any other spot on earth. To Protestant England it was not only, as Lord Curzon said, 'the holiest space of ground on the face of the globe', the land of the Scriptures, the land of the Crusades, the land to which all our faces are turned when we are finally laid in our graves in the churchyard'. It was also the geographical junction between East and West, the bridge head between three continents, the focal point in the strategy of empire . . . .

Few countries attract so much media coverage, or arouse such intense religious feeling and political controversy. Yet it has been the same for countless generations. Why have people for millennia, longed to live here or make a pilgrimage to this land? What is the fascination this land has over so many people around the world?

Someone once described the Holy Land as 'the fifth gospel'. This book aspires to give you a glimpse into the world of that fifth gospel. Through brief notes and stunning pictures the book explains why there is a yearning among many Christians to see the Holy Land, at least once in their lifetime. Local Christians like to call it 'the Land of the Holy One' for it is here we believe that God came to dwell with us and make himself known uniquely in Jesus Christ. It was here that heaven and earth, eternity and time met in the person of Jesus. Many testify to having encountered him in a deeper way at one or more of these places.

You may have never contemplated visiting the Holy Land. You may be thinking about it and want to read something in preparation. Perhaps you travel there regularly. Whatever your situation, these chapters are designed to inform your mind, stir your heart and deepen your faith.

DONKEY, MOUNT OF OLIVES

Aiming to cover the geography, history and biblical significance, you are given an introduction to twenty-one of the most important places that feature in the Bible. Reflect on each location and use the biblical references offered to dig deeper into the Scriptures and see how God has used each place within his providential purposes. Discover how these places have an abiding message today, and may you develop a deeper love for the One who was predicted, born, and lived, died and rose here for you.

If this book has whetted your appetite for more, then at the back you will find advice on recommended further reading and also addresses to write to for more information about the Christian communities and agencies serving in the Holy Land.

Stephen Sizer

SOLOMON'S PILLARS, TIMNA PARK

SUNRISE, SEA OF GALILEE

Samaria

Now [Jesus] had to go through Samaria. So he came to a town in Samaria called Sychar, near the plot of ground Jacob had given to his son Joseph. Jacob's well was there, and Jesus, tired as he was from the journey, sat down by the well. It was about the sixth hour. (John 4:4–6)

Samaria means 'a watch-mountain' or 'watch-tower'. This apposite name refers to the mountainous region, sandwiched between the secular Galilee of the Gentiles in the north and the religious orthodoxy of Jerusalem and Judea to the south. The name was also given to the

hilltop city founded by King Omri, the father of Ahab, after the former owner Shemer, whose name means 'watch' (1 Kings 16:24). This imposing location became the capital of the northern kingdom after Solomon's death. Samaria is a beautiful and diverse region of mountains and valleys.

With good supplies of rain, olives grow in abundance along with vines, grain and citrus fruits. Strategically situated on important ancient highways near the ancient well dug by Jacob, the city of Samaria gave access to Jerusalem to the south, Megiddo and the Jezreel Valley to the north, as well as to the sea and coastal plain to the west, and the Jordan Valley and Phoenicia to the east.

Under the influence of Jezebel and Ahab, Samaria became a notorious centre for idolatrous worship. The Hebrew Prophets repeatedly called on the people of Samaria to repent, graphically warning of judgement for their pride and arrogance (Isaiah 9:8–17), their wickedness (Hosea 7:1–7), rebellion (Hosea 13:16), and exploitation of the poor (Amos 3:9–12; 4:1–3). The city was destroyed and rebuilt on many occasions, its population deported and resettled by waves of Assyrians, Greeks and Romans. It was this mixed community of Jews and Gentiles, known as Samaritans, who in the Hellenistic period built a replica of the Temple to the Hebrew God on

Mount Gerizim to rival that in Jerusalem. This was later destroyed by John Hyrcanus around 128 BC. It is something of an understatement to say that by the time of Christ, the relationship between the Jews and the Samaritans was strained (Luke 9:51–56; John 8:48–51). The animosity was so deep that the Jews would avoid passing through Samaria on their journeys between Galilee and Judea. They would rather take a wide detour to the east, cross the Jordan River and travel through barren and inhospitable Gentile territory if it meant they could avoid contact with Samaritans.

That is why Jesus' attitude towards Samaritans is so remarkable, so free from the ugly racism as common then as today. Jesus openly rebuked his disciples for their hostility towards the Samaritans when rejected by them (Luke 9:55–56). On one memorable occasion Jesus told a story that exalted a Samaritan for his compassion in contrast to the indifference of representatives of his own people (Luke 10:25–37).

On another occasion it was a Samaritan leper whom he praises for his thankfulness, lamenting the ungratefulness of the other nine who were presumably Jews (Luke 17:11–19). Significantly, Jesus intentionally travelled through Samaria (John 4:4), stopped at Jacob's well and asked a Samaritan woman for a drink (John 4:7) to the amazement of his disciples, and then preached the gospel to her community so that many Samaritans responded gladly (John 4:39–42). When in Acts 1:8, the risen Christ commanded his disciples to witness specifically in Samaria, Philip, Peter and John obeyed and many Samaritans came to faith in Jesus Christ (Acts 8:4–17; 15:3).

Samaria, perhaps more than any other location in the Holy Land reminds us of the patience and mercy of God. Its message rebukes our tendency to avoid or discriminate against people because of their race, colour or creed. How often are we, like the disciples, eager to call down fire from heaven upon those who give us a hard time? Samaria emphasises the universality of the gospel and the inclusiveness of God's Kingdom.

THE STEPS OF THE TEMPLE OF AUGUSTUS

WEST GATE, SAMARIA

Beersheba

'Abraham planted a tamarisk tree in Beersheba, and there he called upon the name of the LORD, the Eternal God. And Abraham stayed in the land of the Philistines for a long time.' (Genesis 21:33–34)

Beersheba is an ancient town marking the southern limit of Israeli settlement in biblical times on the northern edge of the Negev Desert. It lies on the trade route to Egypt, midway between Gaza and the Mediterranean Sea to the east and the Dead Sea to the west, about

TAMARISK TREES IN AN OASIS NEAR BEERSHEBA

77 kilometres from Jerusalem to the north. At Beersheba several important personal encounters with God took place. These include Hagar (Genesis 21:8–17); Isaac (Genesis 26:23–33); Jacob (Genesis 46:1–5); and Elijah (1 Kings 19:3).

At Beersheba God taught his people many lessons in how to relate to their neighbours, some of which are still relevant today. It was here that Hagar, the Egyptian servant of Sarah, and her son Ishmael, abandoned by Abraham in the desert, encountered the angel of God. God promised not only that they would survive but that Ishmael would become the father of a great nation (Genesis 21:14–21). This promise was fulfilled in the rise of the Arab peoples. It was also here in the land of the Philistines, living as an alien, that Abraham learnt to call on the name of the Lord. He dug a well and planted a tamarisk tree after agreeing a treaty with Abimelech, king of Gerar over rights to the water (Genesis 21:22–34).

The name Beersheba means 'the well of the seven' and refers to the seven lambs offered as witness to the covenant of mutual assistance between the Patriarch and the Philistines (Genesis 21:31). Beersheba appears to have been the home of Abraham and Isaac, for when the dispute arose between Jacob and Esau over the birthright, it was from

WELL SHAFT

DESERT LANDSCAPE NEAR BEERSHEBA

Beersheba that Jacob began his journey to Mesopotamia in search of a wife (Genesis 28:10). Many years later Jacob, now called Israel, offered sacrifices to God at Beersheba on his way to Egypt to be reunited with his son Joseph (Genesis 46:1). In the times of the Judges, the people of Israel cried out for a king because of the corrupt leadership of Samuel's sons Joel and Abijah at Beersheba (1 Samuel 8:2). When Jezebel tried to kill Elijah he fled to Beersheba and, like Hagar, prayed that he might die there. Here in the desert the Lord sustained Elijah and commissioned him to anoint a new generation of religious and political leaders (1 Kings 19:1–9).

The kingdom in David's time stretched from 'Dan to Beersheba' and this expression came to denote the extent of Israeli settlement from north to south (2 Samuel 17:11). Perhaps because of the associations with the Patriarchs and with the theophanies which occurred there, by the time of Amos, Beersheba had become one of the idolatrous shrines rivalling the true worship of God in Jerusalem. Amos' message remains pertinent when we too are tempted, 'Seek the Lord and live' (Amos 5:4–6; 8:14).

Beersheba reminds us that it is often in our desert experiences, when we are brought low and realise we cannot rely on human resources, that we encounter God afresh. We discover like the Patriarchs did that as we worship him as the one true God of heaven and earth and trust in him alone, he will not only sustain us but give us new direction and purpose.

AN ISRAELITE HOUSE
(ABOVE)

BEDOUIN TENT
(RIGHT)

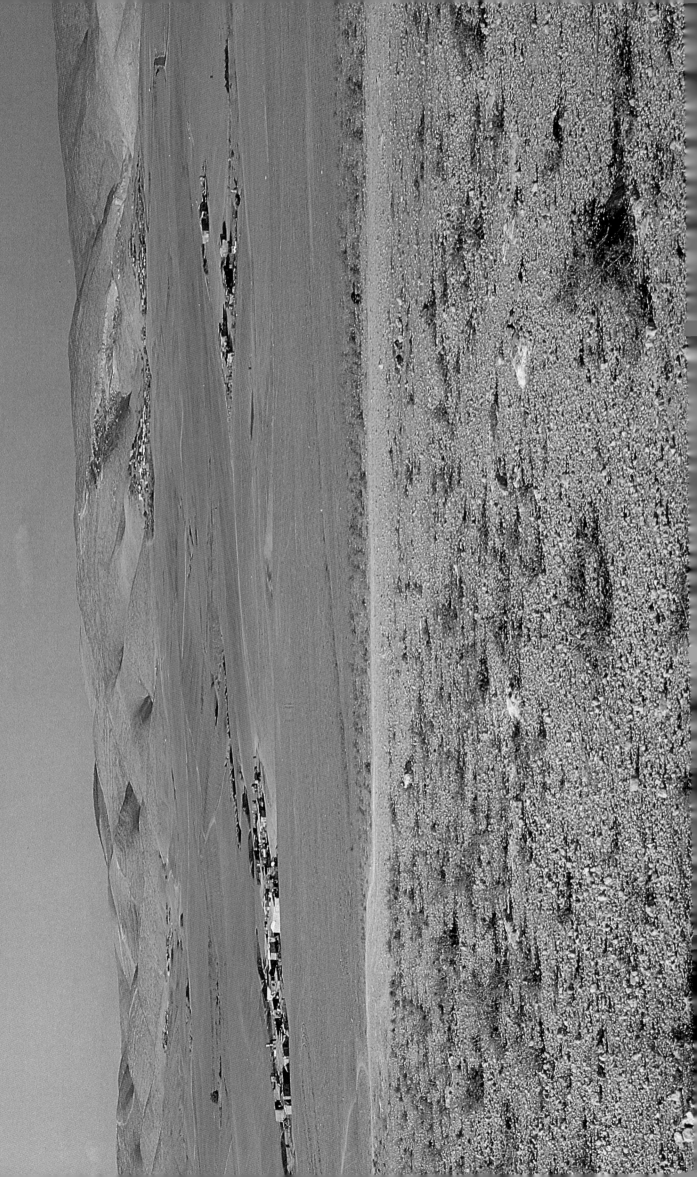

Nazareth

In the sixth month, God sent the angel Gabriel to Nazareth, a town in Galilee, to a virgin pledged to be married to a man named Joseph, a descendant of David. The virgin's name was Mary. (Luke 1:26–27)

Nazareth is nestled in a hollow valley high up among the hills of lower Galilee overlooking the broad and flat Jezreel Valley. It is about halfway between the Sea of Galilee and the Mediterranean.

A GENERAL VIEW OF THE TOWN OF NAZARETH

Caravans on the main trade routes from Egypt, Ptolemais, Gilead and Damascus passed through the valley within a few kilometres of Nazareth. The frequent movement of foreign armies would also have been observed from there at a safe distance. Given its commanding view, it is likely that 'Nazareth' is derived from the Aramaic, meaning 'watch tower' although it is possibly a derivation of the Hebrew for 'shoot'.

Nazareth is not mentioned in either the Old Testament or Talmud. It is first referred to in the Gospels as the home of Mary and Joseph, and the place where Jesus grew up (Matthew 13:53–57; Luke 4:16). Perhaps Joseph felt Jesus would be safe from Archelaus in such a small and relatively obscure community (Matthew 2:21–23). As a growing young man, Jesus met with favour and respect within his community (Luke 2:51–52).

THE FRONT ENTRANCE TO THE STRIKING MODERN CHURCH OF THE ANNUNCIATION

Nazareth may have been regarded as an insignificant or even a dubious place to live, its residents perhaps distinguished by their 'northern' accent. Whatever the reason, Nathaniel is initially scornful when told that the Messiah is from Nazareth (John 1:46). Similarly the religious leaders, not knowing of the birth of Jesus in Bethlehem, were sceptical about his association with Nazareth (John 7:41–43, 52).

Jesus began his public ministry in Nazareth. He had regularly attended the synagogue there but on this occasion, reading from the scroll of Isaiah predicting the coming of the Messiah, Jesus said, 'Today this scripture is fulfilled in your hearing' (Isaiah 61:1–2; Luke 4:16–21). Thinking that they knew him, their response to his claim was one of hostility and rejection (Luke 4:28–30). On a second occasion Jesus returned to his home town and taught in their synagogue (Matthew 13:54–57). But because of their continued unbelief Jesus was unable to perform many miracles (Matthew 13:58). Although known as 'Jesus of Nazareth' (Luke 18:37; 24:19) the saddest day for that community must have been the day Jesus left Nazareth and made Capernaum his home while living in Galilee (Matthew 4:13; 10:13–15).

Nazareth reminds us that it is so easy to despise the familiar; to fail to appreciate or to take for granted things like our homes and families or even God's presence with us. Like the people of Nazareth we may not notice the ways God is intervening in our world, every day, speaking his will into our own personal situations, just as he did that very ordinary day when Mary heard the angel say, 'Greetings, you who are highly favoured! The Lord is with you' (Luke 1:28).

It is not for us to question or try and work out 'how' God's will may be accomplished, but like Mary, our part is to respond in simple trust, 'I am the Lord's servant . . . may it be to me as you have said' (Luke 1:38). And then by God's grace, it most surely will.

HAR NAZARETH, THE HILL JUST OUTSIDE THE TOWN OF NAZARETH

Bethlehem

But you, Bethlehem Ephrathah, though you are small among the clans of Judah, out of you will come for me one who will be ruler over Israel, whose origins are from of old, from ancient times. (Micah 5:2)

The first occasion in which Bethlehem is mentioned in history has been found in the Amarna letters written from tribal kings of Palestine to the Egyptian pharaohs probably sometime between 1400–1360 BC. The ruler in Jerusalem complains that 'Bit-Lahmi' has deserted to the Apiru people, a word probably referring to the Hebrews. Bethlehem is about nine kilometres south of Jerusalem just off the main road to Hebron and Egypt. A strategic position perched 750 metres above sea level, the town sprawls out along several limestone ridges like the tentacles of an octopus. To the east lies Beit Sahour which means the Shepherds Fields and the barren hills of the Judean Desert. To the west are more fertile slopes around Beit Jala where corn and figs, olive fields and vineyards abound.

The town of Bethlehem is mentioned frequently in the Bible. Its location became sacred when Jacob buried his beloved wife Rachel by the roadside near the entrance to Bethlehem (Genesis 35:19; 48:7). It is possible that Salma, the son of Caleb, built the first Jewish settlement there (1 Chronicles 2:51). The town and surrounding fields also feature prominently in the romantic love story of Ruth and Boaz who became the great-grandparents of David (Ruth 1:2:4; 4:11). The town grew in prominence when Samuel anointed the shepherd boy David,

CHURCHES AND MOSQUES CROWD THE CENTRE OF BETHLEHEM

to be king of Israel there (1 Samuel 16:4–13). By New Testament times Bethlehem had come to be known as 'the town of David' (Luke 2:4,11).

Around 700 BC, the prophet Micah predicted that someone greater than David would be born in Bethlehem whose origins, incredibly, would be earlier than his human birth (Micah 5:2). When the Magi came from the East searching for the one to be born king of the Jews, Herod consulted with the chief priests and biblical scholars, who it seems knew full well the significance of Micah's prophecy (Luke 2:1–8; John 7:42).

Bethlehem is therefore unique. It is the place where Almighty God, the Creator of the universe, entered our world and became a human being. It is hard to comprehend the wonder and enormity of this fact. Words cannot improve on the declaration of the angels to the shepherds, 'Today in the town of David a Saviour has been born to you; he is Christ the Lord' (Luke 2:11).

Under the Church of the Nativity, probably the oldest church in the world and best authenticated site in the Holy Land, is a simple

SOLITARY TREE NEAR BETHLEHEM

cave. In the silence of this ancient site, best visited in the early morning, it is possible to pause and worship near the place where the Lord Jesus Christ was born. To enter the church one must first stoop low below the lintel. The tallest must stoop the furthest, only children can enter without bending down. What a lesson in humility.

For many, Bethlehem and the Christmas story is the place where they first begin to experience the meaning of that enigmatic phrase 'He has also set eternity in the hearts of men' (Ecclesiastes 3:11), for here in this place time, eternity and destiny meet in Jesus. Incidentally, in Hebrew, Bethlehem means 'the house of bread'. How appropriate that the One who said 'I am the Bread of Life' should be born in the house of bread. On another occasion Jesus said, 'Whoever eats my flesh and drinks my blood has eternal life, and I will raise him up at the last day. For my flesh is real food and my blood is real drink' (John 6:54–55). Let us indeed feed on him in our hearts by faith with thanksgiving.

Hermon

*It is as if the dew of Hermon were falling on Mount Zion.
For there the LORD bestows his blessing, even life forevermore.*

(Psalm 133:3)

From earliest times Hermon was regarded as a holy place (Psalm 89:12). In Hebrew, Hermon means 'sanctuary', a sacred or forbidden place. It was known as 'Sirion' among the Phoenicians and 'Senir' among the Amorites (Deuteronomy 3:8-9). The mountain was also called 'Baal-Hermon' in the time of Joshua and the Judges, indicating that it was a sacred place of worship prior to the Hebrew conquest (Judges 3:3). Mount Hermon marked the northern boundary for the people of Israel (Joshua 11:16-17; 12:1). The Greeks later worshipped the god Pan there and named the town on its southern slope 'Paneas'. Herod the Great built a marble temple to Augustus Caesar there and Philip the tetrarch renamed the town Caesarea Philippi. In the time of Christ Caesarea Philippi was largely a Gentile frontier town.

SLOPES OF MOUNT HERMON

MOUNT HERMON, SPRINGTIME

Mount Hermon actually comprises three peaks and is the highest mountain in the Levant rising to 2,814 metres. Large quantities of precipitation fall on the mountain, as much as 1,000 metres per year, mostly in the form of snow. The upper slopes remain covered virtually all year. Hermon is the primary source for the Jordan and also feeds the Litani River as well as the Oasis of Damascus. In clear weather, Mount Hermon is visible from great distances. It dominates the landscape. From the Mediterranean Coastal Plain to the Jordan Valley, the snow-capped cone forms the one permanent feature on the northern horizon of Israel. In biblical times the slopes were apparently covered in thick forests, and a home for lions and leopards (Ezekiel 27:5; Song of Songs 4:8).

Mountains like Hermon help give us a wider perspective, and to locate ourselves. They are a security, places associated with retreat and prayer (Mark 3:13). Their age and size make us aware of our own mortality and God's awesome creative power (Psalm 36:5–6). While in exile, David reflected on the depths of the Jordan and the heights of Hermon. They were for him symbols of the source and extent of God's blessing, his love and protection (Psalm 42:5–11; 133:3).

The word used to describe the transfiguration of Jesus is 'metamorphosis'. Amazingly, the same word is used of Christians who are being made like Jesus (Romans 12:1–2). Hermon is a reminder then not only of the transfiguration of Jesus but also of the fact that 'we, who with unveiled faces all reflect the Lord's glory, are being transformed into his likeness with ever-increasing glory' (2 Corinthians 3:18).

Therefore we are not discouraged by adversity for we realise that 'though outwardly we are wasting away, yet inwardly we are being renewed day by day. For our light and momentary troubles are achieving for us an eternal glory that far outweighs them all. So we fix our eyes not on what is seen, but on what is unseen. For what is seen is temporary, but what is unseen is eternal' (2 Corinthians 4:16–18).

MOUNT HERMON AND HULA VALLEY FROM HAR GERSHOM

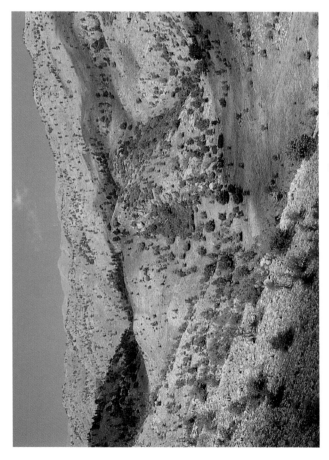

THE ARID SLOPES OF MOUNT HERMON ON THE EASTERN SIDE FACING THE GOLAN HEIGHTS

It is very likely that Mount Hermon is the 'high mountain' on which the Lord Jesus Christ was transfigured (Matthew 17:1–9; Mark 9:2–9; Luke 9:28–37). In the days before, he and his disciples had been ministering in the villages around Caesarea Philippi on the slopes of Mount Hermon. It was also here that Jesus asked his disciples who they thought he was (Matthew 16:13–20). Peter's affirmation that Jesus was indeed 'the Christ, the Son of the Living God' (Matthew 16:16), was then confirmed by the dramatic events on the mountain. Peter, James and John were privileged not only to see the Lord Jesus in his eternal glory but also to hear Almighty God affirm that 'This is my Son, whom I love, with him I am well pleased. Listen to him!' (Matthew 17:5).

Joppa

In Joppa there was a disciple named Tabitha (which, when translated, is Dorcas), who was always doing good and helping the poor. (Acts 9:36)

Joppa, also called Jaffa today, means 'beauty' in Hebrew. It is indeed a beautiful as well as strategic location, set on a rocky outcrop on the Mediterranean coast, the only natural harbour between Egypt and Akko. For this reason it was prized by the Pharoah Thutmose III (c. 1468 BC) as well as Ramases II (c. 1304–1237). In the Amarna letters, for example, the beauty of its gardens are noted as well as the skill of its workers in leather and wood.

It is first mentioned in the Bible as part of the inheritance of the Tribe of Dan (Joshua 19:46), although it largely remained a Philistine stronghold until King David captured it. In the second century

FISHING BOATS IN JOPPA HARBOUR

THE WATERFRONT OF THE OLD TOWN OF JOPPA

BC, conflict between the Maccabees and Greek residents led to its destruction by fire in 142 BC (2 Maccabees 12:3–8). Only then did it become an Israelite town. Pompey captured the town in 63 BC and Antony gave it to Cleopatra of Egypt.

Joppa began to lose its influence as a port when in 22 BC Herod began construction of Caesarea to the north. Joppa had always been a difficult harbour to navigate because of the reefs which form a breakwater about 100 metres off shore. Until the rise of air travel, Joppa remained the main port through which pilgrims passed on their way to the Holy Land.

Joppa is mentioned several times in the Bible. It was to Joppa that rafts of cedarwood from Lebanon were brought for transport overland to Jerusalem for King Solomon to construct the first temple (2 Chronicles 2:16). The same route was used for transporting wood for the second temple commissioned by Cyrus (Ezra 3:7).

Joppa features again in the story of Jonah as the

Phoenician port from which the prophet tried to evade the Lord's commission to preach in the wicked city of Nineveh, later the capital of the Assyrian empire (Jonah 1:3). Jonah had probably grown up to hate the Assyrians and their evil practices (Nahum 3:1–19). His antipathy was so strong that he did not want them to hear of God's mercy (Jonah 4:2–3) even though this had always been God's purpose and Israel's mission (Genesis 12:3; Isaiah 42:6).

In the New Testament, it was also coincidentally in Joppa that the apostle Peter appeared to show a similar reluctance to recognise God's compassion for the Gentiles. Here Peter received a rather less drastic lesson through a vision of various kinds of clean and unclean food (Acts 10:9–16). Peter's vision prepared him to receive the servants of Cornelius who were already on their way from Caesarea to take him back to explain the gospel to the Gentiles. It is interesting that Peter had already chosen to stay in the home of Simon the tanner in Joppa,

since by associating with someone who handled the skins of dead animals he was unclean according to Jewish law. Perhaps Peter's willingness to reject such prejudice helped prepare him for this vision of an inclusive gospel and the realisation that 'God does not show favouritism but accepts men from every nation that fear him and do what is right' (Acts 10:34–35). When the Holy Spirit came upon them in the same way as he had done in Jerusalem on the Day of Pentecost, Peter and the other Jewish believers could no longer view the Gentiles as inferior people excluded from God's saving grace.

Joppa reminds us then of a double lesson: it is futile to run away from God's will, and the proclamation of the good news of Jesus Christ to all people must always be our first priority. We were no more deserving than anyone else, for we are all sinners saved by grace (1 Timothy 2:3–6). This is why there is no place for any distinctions based on race within the Church for, 'There is neither Jew nor Greek, slave nor free, male nor female, for you are all one in Christ Jesus' (Galatians 3:28).

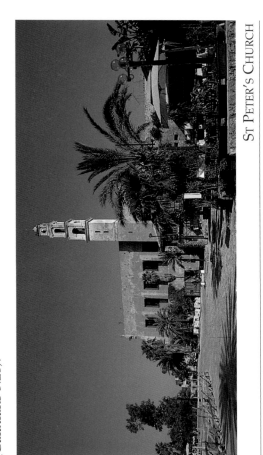

ST PETER'S CHURCH

En Gedi

My lover is to me a cluster of henna blossoms from the vineyards of En Gedi. (Song of Songs 1:14)

A long the western shore of the Dead Sea, the barren hills of the Judean wilderness descend through deep ridges and, for most of the year, dry gullies. Freshwater springs are rare but the most spectacular and abundant is to be found about midway along the shore at En Gedi, some 30 kilometres south-east of Hebron.

Hot water springs burst from the ground about 100 metres above the cliff base forming a beautiful cascading waterfall sustaining a semi-tropical oasis of rich vegetation.

NAHAL ARUGOT WATERFALL,
EN GEDI

DATE PALMS FRINGE THE OASIS AT EN GEDI

Aptly named, En Gedi means 'spring' or 'fountain of the kid'. It was first known as Hazezon Tamar which means 'pruning of palms' suggesting that date palms also once grew here (Genesis 14:7; 2 Chronicles 20:2). En Gedi was inhabited by the Amorites in the days of Abraham (Genesis 14:7), was allotted to Judah (Joshua 15:62), and in the reign of Solomon was renowned for its vineyards (Song 1:14). It was also an important source of aromatic and medicinal plants including henna and balsam. Archaeological remains dated to the time of Josiah (c. 639–609 BC) show evidence that perfumes were produced here.

En Gedi is probably remembered most of all for being the place of refuge where David hid from King Saul and his army of 3,000 men (1 Samuel 23:29–24:1). There are many caves in the area of En Gedi and on one occasion the rugged terrain enabled David to take advantage of Saul who had entered a cave to relieve himself. David's men took this as a providential sign that they should kill Saul (1 Samuel 24:4). This would have secured David's claim to the throne, already confirmed by Samuel (1 Samuel 16:13). David, however, resisted the temptation. In his conscience he knew that such an action was wrong. It was not cowardice but courage David displayed in refusing to kill Saul. He acknowledged that God had appointed Saul and God alone would judge between them, vindicating David at the right time (1 Samuel 24:12–15, 26:10–11).

It was an important lesson David learnt about patience and trusting in the revealed character of God. Perhaps David shared this experience with his son Solomon for he later wrote, 'The king's heart is in the hand of the LORD; he directs it like a watercourse wherever he pleases' (Proverbs 21:1).

The events of David's experience in En Gedi remind us not to interpret our own circumstances too quickly or necessarily read into them God's providence, even when the advice of others coincides. The ends rarely justify the means. Instead we should weigh our circumstances carefully in the light of our conscience and above all in the light of God's word. We should not compromise our moral standards by giving in to group pressure or by taking the easy way out. David used those times alone with God to meditate on God's character and promises. The best way to develop a similar intimacy with God is to take time alone with him and with an open Bible find nourishment and refreshment at your very own spiritual En Gedi. The Psalms, many of which were inspired in this region, are a good place to start (see Psalms 18; 54; 56–57; 59; 63; 142).

WATERFALL AT EN GEDI

The Dead Sea

He said to me, 'This water flows towards the eastern region and goes down into the Arabah, where it enters the Sea. When it empties into the Sea, the water there becomes fresh. Swarms of living creatures will live wherever the river flows. There will be large numbers of fish, because this water flows there and makes the salt water fresh; so where the river flows everything will live.' (Ezekiel 47:8–9)

A PALM TREE ON THE NORTHERN
EDGE OF THE SEA

The Dead Sea marks the lowest point on earth and formed Israel's eastern border. In the Bible it is called by various names including the Salt Sea (Genesis 14:3); the Sea of the Arabah (Joshua 3:16); and the Eastern Sea (Ezekiel 47:18). The Middle East is dominated by a geological fault line which runs from Syria down to Central Africa. The Dead Sea is at the southern end of the Jordan Valley which has been shaped by this fault line. The water level is around 390 metres or 1,300 feet below sea level. The size of the Dead Sea has changed a great deal in history. Today it is approximately 80 kilometres from north to south and 15 kilometres from east to west. In recent years it has been shrinking due to the removal of water from the Jordan River for irrigation. Because there is no outlet for the water, evaporation leaves behind large quantities of mineral deposits such as potash, bromine, magnesium chloride, and other salts, making the Dead Sea, at around 30 per cent solid, the source of the richest mineral deposits on earth. The region also suffers from an inhospitable climate reaching 43°C in summer with an average rainfall of only 5 cm per year.

The shores of the Dead Sea feature in many biblical events. It is believed that the cities of Sodom and Gomorrah were situated near its southern shores (Genesis 13:10–12; 19:24). On its western side the freshwater spring of En Gedi provided a place of refuge for David, when hiding from Saul (1 Samuel 24:1–2); To the south, in the Valley

THE DESOLATE BARRENNESS OF THE DEAD SEA

John refers to the same glorious hope in his vision of Revelation 22. Jesus gave new meaning to the phrase 'living water' in his conversation with the woman at the well of Samaria in John 4 and later in his teaching in the temple itself in John 7.

'On the last and greatest day of the Feast, Jesus stood and said in a loud voice, "If anyone is thirsty, let him come to me and drink. Whoever believes in me, as the Scripture has said, streams of living water will flow from within him"' (John 7.37–38).

There are times perhaps when we can identify with the psalmist David who cried out when he was in the Judean wilderness near the Dead Sea, 'O God, you are my God, earnestly I seek you; my soul thirsts for you, my body longs for you, in a dry and weary land where there is no water' (Psalm 63:1). The good news is we don't have to visit the shores of the Dead Sea to develop a thirst for the living water, the filling of the Holy Spirit, whom Jesus promised to all who seek him.

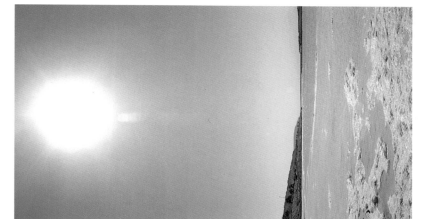

A FIERCE SUN BEATS DOWN RELENTLESSLY ON THE DEAD SEA

DEAD SEA JORDAN RIFT VALLEY (OVERLEAF)

SALT ACCRETIONS FRINGE MOST OF THE DEAD SEA

of Salt, David was victorious over the Edomites (1 Chronicles 18:12–13) as was Jehoshaphat at the Path of Ziz just north of En Gedi (2 Chronicles 20:1–3, 15–17). Herod the Great built one of his fortresses at Machaerus in Perea overlooking the eastern shores of the Dead Sea. It was here that John the Baptist was later imprisoned and beheaded by Herod Antipas (Mark 6:14–29).

Although the Dead Sea is associated, as its name suggests, with death and barrenness, the prophet Ezekiel saw a wonderful vision of a river flowing out from the temple sanctuary in Jerusalem and down through the Judean wilderness into the Dead Sea (Ezekiel 47:1–12). The prophet Zechariah also prophesied, 'On that day living water will flow out from Jerusalem, half to the eastern sea and half to the western sea, in summer and in winter' (Zechariah 14:8). The apostle

Galilee

Nevertheless, there will be no more gloom for those who were in distress. In the past he humbled the land of Zebulun and the land of Naphtali, but in the future he will honour Galilee of the Gentiles, by the way of the sea, along the Jordan – The people walking in darkness have seen a great light; on those living in the land of the shadow of death a light has dawned. (Isaiah 9:1–2)

There were three Roman provinces in Jesus' day, Galilee, Samaria and Judea (Acts 9:31). Galilee was the most northerly of these, extending from Mount Hermon in the north to the Carmel range in the south, and from the Mediterranean coast in the west to the Jordan River in the east.

Galilee may be divided into two separate regions. Upper Galilee lies to the north of a line from the Bay of Acco to the Sea of Galilee

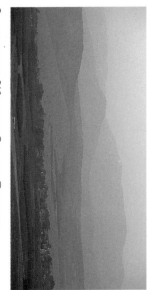

LANDSCAPE WEST OF SEA OF GALILEE

where the hills rise beyond 1,000 metres above sea level. In the days of Christ this region was densely wooded with only a few towns. Lower Galilee which includes the Jezreel Valley is less hilly,

WESTERN SHORES, SEA OF GALILEE

averaging between 500 to 700 metres above sea level. Here the climate is milder, the soil richer and the population was more dense. Josephus mentions that in his day there were 204 villages in Galilee.

Galilee is first mentioned in history following the capture of 23 Canaanite towns by Pharaoah Thutmose III in 1468 BC. Galilee first appears in the Bible with reference to 'The king of Goyim in Gilgal' (Joshua 12:23), probably best translated 'king of the nations of Galilee' indicating the presence of distinct ethnic groups living in the area. Into Galilee came the Israelite tribes of Naphtali, Asher, Issachar and Zebulun, and later, Dan. When Solomon needed to pay Hiram for supplies of wood and gold used in the construction of the temple in Jerusalem, he offered him 20 towns in Galilee as collateral. Hiram did not regard them of sufficient value and it appears Solomon later settled his debt and recovered the towns when his reserves had been replenished (1 Kings 9:10–14; 2 Chronicles 8:1–2). Around 732 BC Tiglath-Pileser, the king of Assyria, deported the Israelites living in Galilee replacing them with people from Babylon and Syria (2 Kings 15:29; 17:24).

It was for this reason that Isaiah describes the area as 'Galilee of the Gentiles', because it was a cosmopolitan mix of Jews, Aramaeans, Ituraeans, Phoenicians and Greeks (Isaiah 9:1; Matthew 4:15). Just prior to the Roman conquest of Palestine in 63 BC, Aristobulus had compelled these communities to adopt Jewish religious customs and keep the Jewish law. He was not very successful and Galilee developed a reputation for independence and rebellion against authority (Luke 13:1; Acts 5:37). It is not surprising therefore that Galileans evolved their own distinctive accent (Matthew 26:69, 73) and had come to be despised by the more orthodox Jews of Judea in the south. When Nicodemus attempted to ensure Jesus received a fair hearing before the Sanhedrin (see Deuteronomy 1:16–17), they replied sarcastically, 'Are you from Galilee too? Look into it and you will find that a prophet does not come out of Galilee' (John 7:52). Their contempt for Galileans distorted their reading of history for at least one prophet, Jonah, and probably Nahum and Hosea also came from Galilee.

It is significant therefore that Jesus chose to fulfil most of his ministry in Galilee. The hills and villages of Galilee provide a vivid backdrop for much of the gospel story. Capernaum, for instance, became his home town (Matthew 9:1). Apart from Judas Iscariot, all his other disciples were Galileans (Matthew 4:18–22; Acts 1:11; 2:7). Jesus performed his first miracle at the wedding in Cana and his last by the Sea of Galilee (John 2:11; 21:4–12). Indeed 25 of his 33 recorded miracles were performed there. Similarly 19 out of 32 of his parables

were spoken in Galilee. This may have been because Galilee gave Jesus access to the rest of the Roman Empire and beyond, through the important trade routes which bisected the region. Galilee also enjoyed comparative freedom from the priestly and pharisaical prejudice found in Jerusalem. Before sending his disciples into the world, after his resurrection Jesus told them to return to their familiar Galilee where he met them by the lakeside.

Galilee was a microcosm of the world. Jesus made his home there, trained his disciples and planned his mission to reach that world from the 'Galilee of the Gentiles'. It is tempting to think that if only our circumstances were different, or we were living in another town or country, we could serve the Lord more effectively. The fact is we must start by living out our faith where we are known, at home. That is where we too will encounter the risen Christ.

Hills ABOVE Sea OF Galilee

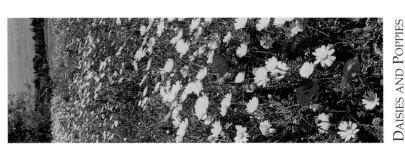

DAISIES AND POPPIES

SEA OF GALILEE FROM THE MOUNT OF BEATITUDES

The Sea of Galilee

As Jesus was walking beside the Sea of Galilee, he saw two brothers, Simon called Peter and his brother Andrew. They were casting a net into the lake, for they were fishermen. 'Come, follow me,' Jesus said, 'and I will make you fishers of men.' (Matthew 4:18–19)

The Sea of Galilee is known by four different names in the Bible. In the Old Testament it is first called the 'Sea of Kinnereth' probably because it is harp-shaped (Numbers 34:11; Joshua 12:3). In the New Testament Luke alone calls it the 'Lake of Gennesaret' (Luke 5:1). Matthew and Mark call it the 'Sea of Galilee' and John twice calls it the 'Sea of Tiberias' (John 6:1; 21:1). The Sea of Galilee, at 211 metres below sea level, is the lowest freshwater lake in the world. At its widest the lake is 13 kilometres from east to west and 22 kilometres from north to south, forming part of the geological fault which runs from Syria to Africa. Within this rift, the River Jordan flows down from Mount Hermon bringing fresh water into the Sea of Galilee near Capernaum on the northern shore and flows out in the south near Yardenit on its way to the Dead Sea.

Hills surround the lake like a horseshoe on the west, north and eastern sides. These are between 360 and 450 metres high and, because the lake is itself below sea level, abrupt changes in temperature can occur. This causes strong winds to sweep down without warning,

BOAT ON THE SEA OF GALILEE

SUNSET, SEA OF GALILEE

Empire. Jesus chose Simon Peter and his brother Andrew, together with James and his brother John from among the fishermen of Galilee to be his disciples. He promised they would become 'fishers of men' (Matthew 4:18–22; Luke 5:1–11). The Sea of Galilee is associated with some of the most dramatic miracles Jesus performed, such as the stilling of the storm (Matthew 8:23–27), the feeding of the 5,000 (Matthew 14:15–21), and the exorcism of the demoniac of Gerasene (Luke 8:26–39). Here too, by the lakeside, the Lord revealed himself to the disciples after his resurrection (John 21). Jesus made use of a fishing net to illustrate what it will be like on the day of judgement when the kingdom of heaven is revealed (Matthew 13:47–50) as had the prophet Ezekiel previously (Ezekiel 32:3). The Sea of Galilee was indeed the cradle of the gospel.

The hills surrounding the Sea of Galilee are spectacular, and it is easy to imagine Jesus with you there, especially when the sun is shining, glittering on the surface of the lake. But you don't have to visit the Sea of Galilee to discover that Jesus is with you and able to still your storms today. Simply see your circumstances, however bleak, from his perspective; allow him full command of your situation; obey his Word and witness his miraculous intervention.

leading to violent storms and turbulent waves. The Gospels record several storms which Jesus and the disciples encountered while on the lake (Matthew 8:23–27; 14:22–34).

In the first century AD the great abundance of fish and shellfish found in the lake attracted a large population in an almost continuous belt of settlements along its northern shore. Important fishing towns of more than 15,000 residents included Capernaum and Bethsaida, which means 'house of fish'. Conveniently, the Via Maris, the international highway from Egypt to Syria, passed along the northern shore near Capernaum. Around 40 different varieties of fish live in the lake. The most popular, Tilapia, is better known now as 'Peter's fish' and these other species were salted and exported all over the Roman

SUNRISE, SEA OF GALILEE

Caesarea

Then Peter began to speak: 'I now realise how true it is that God does not show favouritism but accepts men from every nation who fear him and do what is right.' (Acts 10:34–35)

ROMAN THEATRE, CAESAREA

Caesarea is on the Mediterranean coast between the ancient cities of Jaffa and Dor, on the main coastal road between Tyre and Egypt. Because of the lack of any natural harbour between Sidon and Egypt, the Sidonian king Abdashtart built a fortified anchorage in the fourth century BC. It was called Strabo's Tower after the Greek translation of his name. It became a Greek settlement from 332 BC when Alexander the Great conquered Palestine. During what was a turbulent period it was controlled briefly by the Hasmonean ruler Alexander Jannaeus from 96 BC before Pompey took it in 63 BC. It was then given to Cleopatra by Mark Anthony, but when Octavian Augustus won the battle of Actium in 30 BC he gave the town as a gift to Herod the Great.

Herod took twelve years between 25 and 13 BC to build a magnificent new capital city and harbour based on Hellenistic architecture. He built palaces, a hippodrome, a theatre, an amphitheatre overlooking the sea, a sewer system and an aqueduct which brought water from Mount Carmel. The harbour was a massive engineering project protected by two long semicircular breakwaters 65 metres wide to the north and south of the entrance. These were constructed with giant mortared stones each more than 15 metres long, 5 metres wide and nearly 3 metres deep, which were sunk to a depth of twenty fathoms. Giant statues were erected at the entrance depicting Augustus and Roma. An inner harbour was dug into the shore to enable ships to berth next to vaulted warehouses.

Herod renamed the city Caesarea Maritima since his patron had become Caesar Augustus. The port itself was named Limen Sebastos. Caesarea was the capital of the Roman province of Judea for over 600 years. It was also the headquarters for the Roman army occupying Palestine. It was in Caesarea that King Herod Agrippa I, grandson of Herod the Great, was struck down by an angel for accepting the

ROMAN AQUEDUCT
CAESAREA

The history of Christian witness in Caesarea teaches us that God can use opposition, persecution and even the imprisonment of his servants to spread the gospel. We must not be discouraged by adversity or intimidated by hostility. The gospel cannot be chained or silenced. The blood of the martyrs is indeed the seed of the Church.

THE REMAINS OF THE CRUSADER CITADEL AND HARBOUR, CAESAREA

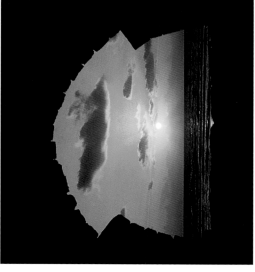

ROMAN AQUEDUCT AT SUNSET, CAESAREA

acclaim of the people that he was divine (Acts 12:19–23). It may also have been divine retribution for executing James, the brother of the apostle John, and for persecuting the Church (Acts 12:1–18).

Caesarea was the strategic focal point in Palestine for the spread of the gospel to the Gentile world. It is remembered as the place where God led a reluctant Peter to share the good news of Jesus Christ with the Roman centurion Cornelius and his family. They became the first Gentiles to believe and be baptised in the name of Jesus Christ (Acts 10:1–8, 22–48). Philip the evangelist, who led the Ethiopian eunuch to Christ, also lived in Caesarea with his four daughters (Acts 8:26–40; 21:8–9).

Paul used the port of Caesarea to escape to Tarsus after threats were made to kill him in Jerusalem (Acts 9:30). He also landed at Caesarea after both his second and third missionary journeys (Acts 18:22; 21:8). Later, Paul was held as a prisoner in Caesarea for two years (Acts 23:31–26:32). There, while on trial, God gave Paul the opportunity to make his defence of the Christian faith before the Roman governor Antonius Felix (Acts 24:1–26); his successor, Porcius Festus (Acts 25:1–22); and also King Herod Agrippa II (Acts 25:23–26:32). From Caesarea Paul was eventually taken to Rome having appealed to be tried before Caesar.

Jericho

There are three sites on which Jericho was built at different times in history. The conical mound of Tel Jericho represents all that remains of the earliest settlements. Just to the east where the Wadi Qelt emerges from the Judean wilderness into the Jordan Valley lie the foundations of first-century Jericho with its royal winter palaces of the Hasmonean and Herodian period. Modern Crusader Jericho is a short walk to the south and is visible for great distances because of the abundance of its trees and rich green vegetation.

Jericho is situated in the broad and fertile Jordan Plain, opposite Mount Nebo (Deuteronomy 32:49), ten kilometres north of the Dead Sea and at 240 metres below sea level, the lowest city on earth. The climate is tropical, which, combined with the rich alluvial soil, the presence of a perennial spring and the proximity of the Jordan River, has created an oasis justly earning Jericho the accolade 'city of palms' (Deuteronomy 34:3). A historic east–west road which fords the River Jordan nearby also makes Jericho a strategic entry point into Palestine (Joshua 3:14–17). It is probably for these reasons that Jericho is the

JERICHO FROM MONASTERY OF TEMPTATION

Then they came to Jericho. As Jesus and his disciples, together with a large crowd, were leaving the city, a blind man, Bartimaeus (that is, the Son of Timaeus), was sitting by the roadside begging. When he heard that it was Jesus of Nazareth, he began to shout, 'Jesus, Son of David, have mercy on me!' (Mark 10:46–47)

NEOLITHIC STONE TOWER (8000 BC)

VIEW OVER JERICHO

53

Jesus visited Jericho on a number of occasions. The traditional site where he was baptised by John in the Jordan River is near Jericho (Matthew 3:5–17). Similarly his temptation may have taken place in the Judean wilderness to the west of the city (Matthew 4:1–11). Jewish pilgrims travelling to Jerusalem from Galilee who wished to avoid Samaria would travel via Jericho. On occasions Jesus also used this route (Matthew 20:17–19; 20:29–21:2). In Jericho Jesus called people like Zacchaeus, the tax collector, to become his disciples, and demonstrated his Messianic claims and supernatural power by giving sight to the blind (Mark 10:46–52). Some of his parables such as of 'the Good Samaritan' were inspired by the dramatic scenery, and in this case, the hazardous road between Jericho and Jerusalem (Luke 10:30).

Jericho stands as testimony to the power of faith. Trusting in God may indeed see walls brought down (Hebrews 11:30); sight received (Mark 10:52); prejudice overcome (Luke 10:30–33); human nature transformed (Luke 19:9–10).

JERICHO,
JORDAN RIFT VALLEY

oldest known inhabited city in the world. The earliest remains are dated to around 7,000 years BC so that by the time the Hebrew tribes emerged from the wilderness, Jericho was already an ancient and prosperous city defended by stone walls built on an earthen embankment. The name Jericho is associated with the worship of the semitic fertility cult moon-god Yarih.

Given its strategic location, the most important settlement in the Jordan Valley, Jericho features prominently in the story of the settlement of Palestine by the Israelites. After Jericho was destroyed by the Israelites, no attempt was made to rebuild the city for 400 years and the site remained uninhabited (Joshua 6:24–26). During this long period of abandonment the remains of the fallen city walls and buildings were exposed to the weather and eroded, making their dating within the archaeological strata difficult. Jericho was eventually rebuilt by Hiel of Bethel in the reign of King Ahab. The curse placed by Joshua on anyone re-establishing the city was fulfilled in the death of his eldest and youngest sons (1 Kings 16:34). In the time of Elijah and Elisha, Jericho was the home for a school of prophets (2 Kings 2:4–5, 18–22). The plains of Jericho also feature in the sad story of the capture of Zedekiah, the last king of Judah, by the Babylonians (2 Kings 25:5-7).

WATERFALL NEAR BANYAS, GOLAN HEIGHTS

River Jordan

Lot looked up and saw that the whole plain of the Jordan was well watered, like the garden of the LORD, like the land of Egypt, toward Zoar: (Genesis 13:10)

In Hebrew, Jordan (Yarden), means 'the descender'. This is because it flows through the Jordan Valley from the snowy slopes of Mount Hermon, the highest peak in the Orient, down to the Dead Sea, the lowest place on earth. It is also the lowest river on earth, flowing for most of its course below sea level. Whereas the distance from Mount Hermon to the Dead Sea is 113 kilometres, the length of the Jordan River, as it meanders through the valley, is actually 323 kilometres.

The Jordan has three principle sources: the first is the Leddan which flows from the base of the hillside near the ancient border town of Dan. The second source, called the Banias, flows from under the limestone cliffs near the ruins of Caesarea Philippi joining the Leddan about nine kilometres south of Dan. The third source is called the Hasbany which rises on the western slopes of Mount Hermon and joins the main stream about two kilometres further south. Here the river is about 15 metres wide and flows through a deep channel 4 to 5 metres deep before it enters the Sea of Galilee. For most of its length the Jordan is between 28 and 31 metres wide and between 1 and 3 metres deep. Because there are 27 sets of rapids along the river it carries no traffic. Although there were a number of fords between the Sea of Galilee and the Dead Sea, it was not until the arrival of the Romans that the river was bridged.

There are two important tributaries which enter the River Jordan further south, between the Sea of Galilee and the Dead Sea. The Yarmuk formed the boundary between Bashan and Gilead, and the Jabbok which enters the Jordan about 30 kilometres north of Jericho was formerly the northern boundary of Ammon.

Led by Joshua, the Israelites miraculously crossed the flooded Jordan, probably near Adam, 26 kilometres north of Jericho, 'on dry land' (Joshua 3:15–17). God later enabled both Elijah and Elisha to repeat the miracle (2 Kings 2:8,14). Naaman was healed in its waters (2 Kings 5:8–14) and David crossed it to escape from his rebellious son Absalom (2 Samuel 17:22–24). The importance of the Jordan River in Scripture is because it was regarded as a natural border, not just between the eastern and western tribes of Israel (Numbers 34:10–12), but also, as now, as a military frontier (Judges 7:24; 12:5). In the New Testament, the River Jordan features most significantly in the ministry of John the Baptist and in the baptism of the Lord Jesus (Matthew 3:6; Mark 1:9–11).

To cross the Jordan became figurative of making a decision, like crossing the Rubicon (Deuteronomy 3:18–20; 27:4; Joshua 1:2). Is there a 'Jordan' that you must cross metaphorically, in obedience to God, in order that you too may experience his blessings and receive your inheritance?

JORDAN RIVER, SOUTH OF SEA OF GALILEE

JORDAN RIVER, NORTH OF SEA OF GALILEE

Surrounded by mountains, the entire valley is in a rain shadow from the westerly rain-bearing winds. Average annual rainfall at Dan is about 600 mm. The Sea of Galilee receives about 400 mm, whereas at Jericho on average only 125 mm falls each year. In biblical times the Jordan Valley was full of dense vegetation and in many places was also swampy, the habitat of lions and other wild animals (Jeremiah 12:5; 50:44; Zechariah 11:3). It is probably for a combination of these reasons that no large city ever grew up on the banks of the Jordan.

The Jordan did however play a significant role in the history of Israel and is mentioned 178 times in the Old Testament and 15 in the New Testament. It is first referred to in the story of Abraham and Lot when they separated and shared the land between them (Genesis 13:8–12). Jacob crossed the Jordan on several occasions (Genesis 32:10), wrestling with the Lord at the ford of the Jabbok (Genesis 32:22–30).

THE RIVER
JORDAN AS IT
FLOWS INTO THE
SEA OF GALILEE

The Judean Wilderness

'I will make rivers flow on barren heights, and springs within the valleys. I will turn the desert into pools of water, and the parched ground into springs. I will put in the desert the cedar and the acacia, the myrtle and the olive . . . so that people may see and know, may consider and understand, that the hand of the LORD has done this, that the Holy One of Israel has created it.' (Isaiah 41:18–20)

The Judean wilderness roughly extends from the shores of the Dead Sea, west through the mountainous central plateau before it begins to descend to the coastal plains near Gaza by the Mediterranean Sea (Judges 1:16). To the south lies the more inhospitable wilderness of Sinai (Exodus 19:1) and to the north, Jerusalem and the hills of Samaria. The word Judea is the Greco-Latin form of Judah. The term Judah was used by Ezra to describe the area of Palestine around Jerusalem which

was then under Persian rule (Ezra 5:8). There are only three natural springs on the eastern edge of the Judean wilderness, at Jericho, Ain Feshka, 16 kilometres to the south, and at En Gedi another 28 kilometres further south.

The word used to describe this wilderness in Hebrew is midbar, meaning 'pasture-ground' and denotes land without settled inhabitants or natural sources of water. The word is also used to describe the wilderness between Egypt and Palestine where the tribes of Israel wandered with their flocks and herds for 40 years (Exodus 19:2; Jeremiah 2:6). This area is known as a 'tame desert' because of its latent fertility needing only water to make it fruitful. It receives limited rainfall of between 100–300 millimetres a year, although

JUDEAN DESERT NEAR WADI QELT (NAHAL PERAT)

returning the earth to its primeval chaos as it was before creation (Jeremiah 4:23–26).

NAHAL PERAT, JUDEAN DESERT

amounts can vary dramatically from year to year. The wilderness of Judea is prone to sudden storms causing dangerous flash floods which tend to occur in March or April. The erosion caused by these floods leave a dramatic mark on the landscape. For a matter of only a few weeks, when rain has fallen, the Judean wilderness is carpeted in a brief but beautiful display of flowers and greenery (Isaiah 35:1–2).

The Bible depicts the desert as the habitat of raiders such as the Amalekites and Midianites who

WADI QELT (NAHAL PERAT)

frequently attacked the Israelite farmers. They were sent by God to punish the Jews for rebelling against him (Judges 6:1–6). Saul was eventually able to provide some measure of relief from these attacks (1 Samuel 14:47–48). It was here that David shepherded his father's flocks (1 Samuel 17:28; 26:1–3) and found refuge from Saul (1 Samuel 23:21–29). Two of the prophets were born here, Amos at Tekoa and Jeremiah at Anathoth. John the Baptist also lived and preached in the Judean wilderness (Luke 1:80; 3:1–6).

The inhospitable desert was held in fear and awe by the Jews, a place of terror (Isaiah 21:1). The Israelites were warned to remember how the Lord protected them from its harsh climate and 'venomous snakes and scorpions' when later they were tempted to become proud and arrogant (Deuteronomy 8:10–20). Figuratively, the desert was also used to depict the graphic effects of God's judgement (Isaiah 33:8–9),

Mount Sinai

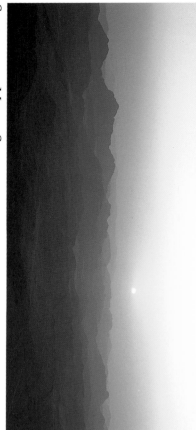

When Moses went up on the mountain, the cloud covered it, and the glory of the LORD settled on Mount Sinai. For six days the cloud covered the mountain, and on the seventh day the LORD called to Moses from within the cloud. To the Israelites the glory of the LORD looked like a consuming fire on top of the mountain. Then Moses entered the cloud as he went on up the mountain. And he stayed on the mountain forty days and forty nights. (Exodus 24:15–18)

SUNRISE FROM MOUNT SINAI

Mount Sinai which is also called Mount Horeb, lies within the Sinai Peninsula, a large wedge-shaped land bridge between Africa and Asia bounded by the Gulf of Suez, the Mediterranean, the Gulf of Aqaba and the Red Sea. The exact location of Mount Sinai is not known but it is believed to be near Ras Sasafeh where the mountain range climbs almost vertically from the Sinai Plain. Dean Stanley, the nineteenth-century explorer describes how the dramatic scenery, '. . . presents a long retiring sweep, within which the people could remove and stand afar off. The cliff, rising like a huge altar in front of the whole congregation, and visible against the sky in lonely grandeur from end to end of the whole plain, is the very image of the "mount that might be touched", and from which the voice of God might be heard far and wide over the plain below.'

Having left Egypt a few months before, the people of Israel journeyed about 240 kilometres and camped in 'the Desert of Sinai' at the foot of the mountain. There they stayed for a whole year (Exodus 19:1–2; Numbers 10:11–13). It was there on Mount Sinai that the Lord God revealed himself through Moses to Israel (Exodus 19:17–24). The Law of God was given (Exodus 20), the role of the Levite priests established (Numbers 3), the first tabernacle built (Numbers 9:15), and the covenant between God and Israel confirmed (Exodus 24). So significant was this event that the mountain came to symbolise God's awesome presence

VIEW FROM MOUNT SINAI AT DAWN

of God by faith through the new covenant (Galatians 4:24–25; Hebrews 12:18–24). It was actually God, not Moses, who provided food and water for the Israelites in the wilderness (John 6:32). Paul even asserts that Christ was the very Rock (1 Corinthians 10:4). One greater than Moses has now appeared (Hebrews 3:2–6).

The experience of Israel in the wilderness of Sinai is used as a sober lesson to warn Christians not to commit the same sins of idolatry and unbelief which led to God's judgement (1 Corinthians 10:1–13; Hebrews 3:7–19). We must never become complacent or, worse still, arrogant about the basis of our salvation. The genuineness of our faith in Christ is evidenced not by our profession but by our perseverance.

MOUNT SINAI IS A SUCCESSION OF ARID PEAKS

and protection (Judges 5:4–5; Psalm 68:7–8). The other events that occurred when Israel camped at the foot of Mount Sinai are recorded in Exodus 19–40, Leviticus and Numbers 1–11.

Following his victory over the 450 prophets of Baal at Mount Carmel, Elijah, exhausted and afraid of Jezebel's threats of revenge, fled to Mount Sinai. Here the Lord graciously appeared to him, not in the wind or earthquake, but in the still small voice. Elijah was re-commissioned to anoint two new kings, and Elisha as his successor (1 Kings 19:1–18).

BUSH GROWING IN CLIFF FACE, SOUTH SINAI DESERT

There are also a number of significant references and allusions to Mount Sinai in the New Testament. Like Moses, Jesus spent 40 days alone in the wilderness (Luke 4:1–13). In his transfiguration on another high mountain, Jesus encountered Moses and Elijah both of whom had met with God on Mount Sinai. The shekinah glory of God as well as the voice of God confirmed Christ's authority (Matthew 17:1–5). In another allusion to Mount Sinai, Jesus compares himself with the cursed snake lifted up by Moses to save those being punished for their rebellion (John 3:13–15). After Jesus had been rejected and crucified, Sinai came to be associated with those still in slavery under the old covenant. This is contrasted with those set free to be the true children

Golgotha

At the place where Jesus was crucified, there was a garden, and in the garden a new tomb, in which no one had ever been laid. Because it was the Jewish day of Preparation and since the tomb was nearby, they laid Jesus there. (John 19:41–42)

There are two places associated with Calvary in Jerusalem today. The traditional site has been venerated since before Hadrian (117–138 BC) built a pagan shrine to Venus over the tomb and a statue to Jupiter on Golgotha to eliminate the Christian churches. In 326 BC, Queen Helena, the mother of the emperor Constantine was shown the site by Bishop Macarius, and had the pagan temple demolished. In its place she built the Church of the Holy Sepulchre to encompass both the site of Calvary and the tomb of Jesus.

The other location, north of the Damascus Gate, has been venerated since 1885 when the rather eccentric General Charles Gordon popularised the notion that a rocky hill at the back of a disused quarry appeared to match the skull-like description of Calvary. One of its names, Betha-Sekilah, means 'Place of Stoning'. Its proximity to a tomb discovered in 1849 seemed to corroborate this assertion. The tomb itself may date from the time of Herod Agrippa (AD 37–44), although the doorway and windows appear to be Byzantine or later. Gordon disputed the authenticity of the Church of the Holy Sepulchre because it lies within the walls of Jerusalem. Jews would not bury their dead within a populated area because tombs were regarded as unclean. What Gordon did not appreciate, however, was that the Ottoman walls of the sixteenth century were built further north than those of the first-century Roman Jerusalem so, later, encompassing the area around the Church of the Holy Sepulchre. Evangelical tastes also came to prefer the simplicity of the Garden Tomb to the ornate and complex oriental religious shrines within the Church of the Holy Sepulchre. Scriptures give us some clues as to the location of Calvary.

THE ROCKY OUTCROP RESEMBLING A SKULL WHICH CAUGHT THE EYE OF GENERAL GORDEN

GARDEN TOMB, JERUSALEM

Matthew, Luke and John specifically mention that this was a new tomb in which no one had yet been buried, one that was sealed with a rolling stone (Matthew 27:59–60; Luke 23:50–53; John 19:41). John and the writer of Hebrews emphasise that Jesus was crucified outside the city walls (John 19:20; Hebrews 13:12) while John specifically mentions that the tomb was within a garden (John 19:41). Matthew adds that Jesus was buried in a tomb belonging to Joseph of Arimathea, a wealthy member of the Sanhedrin who had not consented to the execution of Jesus but was himself a secret disciple (Matthew 27:57–60).

The place where Christ was crucified is called Golgotha in the Gospels. This is the transliteration of an Aramaic word meaning 'the place of the skull' (Mark 15:22). The word is also used twice in the Old Testament, literally the skulls of Abimelech and Jezebel (Judges 9:53; 2 Kings 9:35). Our English word 'Calvary' means the same thing and comes from the Latin 'calvaria'. It is probable that the location was given this name because it was a place of execution and a skull symbolised death.

In ancient Palestine, caves were commonly used as graves or tombs. Over several generations, members of the same family would share a cave to bury their deceased. The word 'sepulchre' is translated from the Hebrew and refers to a niche that was carved out

Church of the Holy Sepulchre, Jerusalem

of the side of the cave in which the body of a deceased person would be placed (Genesis 23:6). When only the bones remained they would be gathered and placed at the back of the cave, sometimes in a sarcophagus. Jewish tombs had small niches carved out of the walls in which bodies were placed. First-century examples of these can still be seen at the back of the Syrian chapel within the Church of the Resurrection, ironically named the Tomb of Joseph of Arimathea.

The most significant fact about the tomb of Jesus, however, is not its exact geographical location. What matters is that it was empty. 'He is not here, he is risen' (Luke 24:6). Only after they had encountered the risen Lord did the disciples begin to comprehend his incredible promise, 'I am the resurrection and the life. He who believes in me will live, even though he dies; and whoever lives and believes in me will never die' (John 11:25–26). At Golgotha, heaven and earth unite, where time and eternity meet. The place uniquely demonstrates to us the extent of God's unconditional love, the cost of achieving forgiveness for our sin, and proclaims the assurance of life everlasting. Have you acknowledged that Jesus died in your place in order that you may share his risen life (1 Peter 3:18; Romans 5:8)?

Interior of Garden Tomb (Possible Burial Site of Jesus), Jerusalem

ROCK FACE (SKULL), POSSIBLE GOLGOTHA SITE, JERUSALEM

The Garden
of Gethsemane

They went to a place called Gethsemane, and Jesus said to his disciples, 'Sit here while I pray'. He took Peter, James and John with him, and began to be deeply distressed and troubled. 'My soul is overwhelmed with sorrow to the point of death,' he said to them. 'Stay here and keep watch.' Going a little farther, he fell to the ground and prayed that if possible the hour might pass from him. 'Abba, Father,' he said,

'everything is possible for you. Take this cup from me. Yet not what I will, but what you will.' (Mark 14:32–36)

Gethsemane means 'oil press' in Aramaic and is situated on the Mount of Olives across the Kidron Valley and overlooking the temple of Jerusalem. The various references in the Gospels suggest that this was an enclosed piece of ground which Jesus 'entered' (Matthew 26:36). John very specifically mentions that it was a garden (John 18:1). The exact location is not known since in AD 70 Titus cut down all the trees on the Mount of Olives in his siege of Jerusalem.

Jesus came to the Garden of Gethsemane often to pray alone and to be with his disciples, especially in the evenings leading up to his trial and crucifixion. This may indeed have been the place where he lodged when visiting Jerusalem (Luke 21:37; 22:39). After sharing the Last Supper with his disciples Jesus took them to the Garden of Gethsemane one last time to pray in preparation for his imminent betrayal and arrest (Matthew 26:36–46). Judas, knowing this was where Jesus would be, brought the Jewish religious leaders to arrest him in the Garden (Matthew 26:47–56).

The Bordeaux Pilgrim writing in AD 333 specifically mentions the existence of a vineyard with a rock where Judas betrayed Jesus. The

OLIVE TREE TRUNK

'My Father, if it is not possible for this cup to be taken away unless I drink it, may your will be done' (Matthew 26:38; 42). He was tempted as we are, yet withstood the test and overcame (Hebrews 5:7–9). Therefore we can identify with him as he has done with us. 'Let us fix our eyes on Jesus, the author and perfecter of our faith, who for the joy set before him endured the cross, scorning its shame, and sat down at the right hand of the throne of God. Consider him who endured such opposition from sinful men, so that you will not grow weary and lose heart' (Hebrews 12:2–3).

It is possible that the apostles saw a parallel with the Garden of Eden where the first Adam disobeyed God and sin and death entered the world. Here in another garden the second Adam overcame temptation and by his death in our place brought forgiveness and life (Romans 5:15–17; 1 Corinthians 15:21–22).

If you ever find yourself too tired to pray, or perhaps in dark times have felt unable to pray or been tempted to deny Christ, remember the events in the Garden of Gethsemane. The apostles have been there before you. Like Peter, take a few moments to confess your sin, recommit yourself to follow Christ and hear his words of comfort and love (John 21:15–17; 1 John 1:8–10).

MOUNT OF OLIVES AND GETHSEMANE

first church to commemorate the events of the Garden of Gethsemane at the foot of the Mount of Olives was probably built by Theodosius between 379–384 BC. This was destroyed by the Persians and rebuilt by the Crusaders. Today the Church of All Nations, completed in 1924, stands on the site over the 'rock of agony' on which it is believed Jesus prayed before his arrest. Beside the church is a simple but beautiful garden with eight very old olive trees, the largest of which has a girth of nearly six metres. Olive trees never die so it is possible the trees that survive today have grown from the stumps of those that witnessed the sad events that first Maundy Thursday. Carbon-dating tests carried out in 1982 confirm that some of the wood may be 2,300 years old.

It was in the Garden of Gethsemane, alone, just as in the Judean wilderness at the beginning of his ministry, that Jesus was tempted by Satan. He was overcome with sorrow knowing what lay before him, yet he submitted obediently to the will of God,

Olive Tree,
Israel

The Walls of Jerusalem

The sacrifices of God are a broken spirit; a broken and contrite heart, O God, you will not despise. In your good pleasure make Zion prosper; build up the walls of Jerusalem. (Psalm 51:17–18)

The ancient city of Jerusalem is situated on a spur of land where three deep wadis, the Kidron, Tyropoean and Hinnom, merge to form one valley sloping south towards the Dead Sea. Jerusalem was first settled by the Amorites and Hittites (Ezekiel 16:3,45). Indeed the name 'Jerusalem' means 'founded by the god Shalem' after one of the Amorite gods. Jerusalem's long history is written in its walls as they were built up, seiged, demolished, rebuilt and expanded by its successive inhabitants; so much so that Jerusalem has been the scene of conflict on over 40 occasions during its history.

The earliest walls of ancient settlements were often made of earth or clay bricks mixed with reed. Over time these were vulnerable to erosion from the weather, structural instability or destruction by fire. For this reason they are often difficult to locate or date with certainty (Isaiah 30:13; Amos 1:7,10,14). The earliest known walls of Jerusalem were made of stone and exploited the natural defensible terrain to the east, south and west (Isaiah 2:15; 9:10; Zephaniah 1:16).

Although mentioned in the demarcation of the land taken by Judah and Benjamin (Joshua 18:15), Jerusalem first gained significance to the Israelites when David captured the Jebusite city and made it his capital. He may have done so because it was more central than Hebron to the emerging kingdom formed from the twelve tribes of Israel. David made use of the Jebusite fortifications which may have included only one gate (2 Samuel 15:2). Solomon was probably the first to incorporate the northern hill of Mount Moriah within the city walls having built the temple there around 1010 BC. In 722 BC, with the fall of the northern kingdom, refugees arrived in Jerusalem and

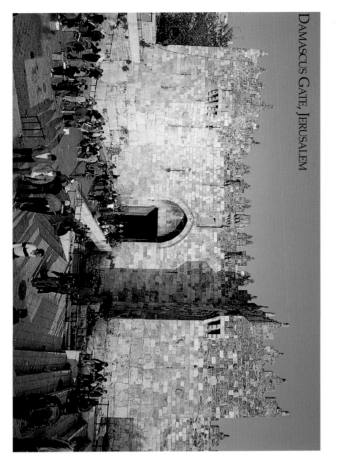

DAMASCUS GATE, JERUSALEM

TORAH SCROLL, WESTERN WALL, JERUSALEM

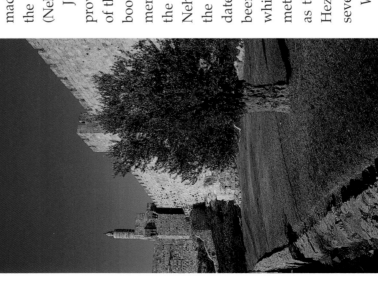

OLD CITY
WALLS AND
CITADEL,
JERUSALEM

Hezekiah enlarged the walls to the west to contain the burgeoning population. These walls were sufficiently impregnable to survive the seige of Sennacherib in 702 BC, and traces remain today (2 Chronicles 32:5). Nebuchadnezzar, the king of Babylon, destroyed the city in 586 BC following a siege that lasted three years (2 Kings 25; Jeremiah 39). The temple and palaces were destroyed by fire and the walls again razed to the ground. These were rebuilt under Ezra and Nehemiah in around 430 BC, following the return of some of the Israelites from exile in Babylon (Nehemiah 2–3). Nehemiah's description of the walls and gates of Jerusalem is the most comprehensive to be found anywhere in the Bible. It is likely that use was made of the existing foundations and that the gates were given their former names (Nehemiah 12:31–39).

Josephus, the Jewish historian, provides us with the most detailed record of the walls of the first century AD in his book *The Jewish Wars*. He specifically mentions three walls which incorporated the work of Solomon, Hezekiah, Nehemiah, the Hasmoneans and Herod the Great. Remains of a wall and tower dated to the seventh century BC have been found under the Roman Cardo which are four metres thick and eight metres high. Another discovery known as the Broad Wall, dated to the work of Hezekiah in the eighth century BC, is seven metres wide.

With the capture of Jerusalem by the Romans, the city witnessed significant changes to its shape and size. In AD 41, for instance, Herod Agrippa doubled the size of the city by building a third wall on the north and west sides of the city which also, incidentally, brought the site of Calvary inside the wall. This was, however, never completed, as the entire city was destroyed in AD 70 by the Romans. Hadrian eventually rebuilt it, including its walls, renaming it Colonia Aelia Capitolina. His work included the enlargement of the northern wall which became 6 metres wide and 13 metres high with 90 towers. The walls of Jerusalem today, with their 35 towers and eight gates, are largely the work of Suleiman the Magnificent and date from the sixteenth century. In places they are built over a patchwork of much earlier walls and gates and the immense layers of rubble accumulated over thousands of years.

In the Bible, walls are used to symbolise many things but especially to describe salvation. It is good to remember that our security should never rest in stone defences but in God alone who is our eternal rock (Isaiah 26:1; 60:18). So often walls are built to exclude or divide people. Jesus Christ has broken down the wall of separation between Jew and Gentile that had once existed in the temple, enabling all people to come to know God through him. It is for us to live out this equal grace and common justice in our divided world (Ephesians 2:14).

LION GATE, JERUSALEM

What Next?

Recommended Further Reading . . . .

1. The History and Archaeology of the Holy Land

Werner Keller, *The Bible as History*, Illustrated Edition (Oxford: Lion Publishing, 1991).

Alan Millard, *A Treasury of Bible Pictures* (Oxford: Lion Publishing, 1987).

2. The Best Guidebooks to the Holy Land

Ronald Brownrigg, *Come See The Place* (London: Hodder and Stoughton, 1988).

Shirley Eber and Kevin O'Sullivan, *The Rough Guide to Israel and the Occupied Territories* (London: Rough Guides, 1992).

Garth Hewitt, *Pilgrims and Peacemakers* (Oxford: Bible Reading Fellowship, 1995).

Norman Wareham and Jill Gill, *Every Pilgrim's Guide to the Holy Land* (Norwich: Canterbury Press, 1996).

Baedeker's Israel (Norwich: Jarrold and Sons (and the AA), 1993).

The Holy Land, Everyman Guides (London: David Campbell Publishers, 1995).

3. The Contemporary Political Situation

Colin Chapman, *Whose Promised Land?* (Oxford: Lion Publishing, 1992).

Kenneth Cragg, *Palestine: The Prize and Price of Zion* (London: Cassell, 1997).

Ron David, *Arabs and Israel for Beginner* (New York: Writers and Readers Publishing, 1993).

Michael Prior, *The Bible and Colonialism* (Sheffield: Sheffield University Press, 1997).

Edward Said, *The Question of Palestine* (London: Vintage, 1992).

Don Wagner, *Anxious for Armageddon* (Scottdale: Herald Press, 1995).

4. The Local Christian Community

Naim Ateek, *Justice and Only Justice* (Maryknoll: Orbis, 1990).

Elias Chacour, *Blood Brothers: A Palestinian's Struggle for Reconciliation in the Middle East* (Eastbourne: Kingsway, 1984).

Elias Chacour, *We Belong to the Land* (London, Marshall Pickering, 1992).

Kenneth Cragg, *The Arab Christian: A History in the Middle East* (London: Cassell, 1992).

Audeh Rantisi, *Blessed are the Peacemakers* (Guildford: Eagle, 1990).

Useful Christian Contacts for the Holy Land . . . .

AMOS TRUST. All Hallows on the Wall, 83 London Wall, London EC2M 5NA Tel: 0171-588-2661. Fax: 0171-588-2663. E-mail: Amos_Trust @Compuserve.com

THE ALTERNATIVE TOURISM GROUP. PO Box 173, Beit Sahour, West Bank. via Israel. Tel: 972-2-6472151. Fax: 972-2-6472211. E-mail: atg@p-ol.com

BETHLEHEM ARAB SOCIETY FOR REHABILITATION. PO Box 100. Bethlehem, West Bank. via Israel. Tel: 972-2-744050

BETHLEHEM BIBLE COLLEGE. Hebron Road, PO Box 127, Bethlehem, West Bank, via Israel. Tel: 972-2-741190. Fax: 972-2-743278

BIBLE LANDS SOCIETY. PO Box 50, High Wycombe, Buckinghamshire. HP15 7QU Tel: 01494 521351

Christ Evangelical Church School, PO Box 75, Nazareth, 16100. Israel. Tel 972-6-6554017. Fax: 972-6-6563649

ECUMENICAL TRAVEL SERVICE. The Middle East Council of Churches. Liaison Office, PO Box 14634, East Jerusalem 91146. via Israel. Tel: 972-2-6284493. Fax: 972-2-6284730

JERUSALEM INTERNATIONAL YMCA, 26 King David Street. PO Box 294, 91002, Jerusalem. Israel. Tel: 972-2-5692680. Fax: 972-2-625438

LIVING STONES, c/o St Mary's University College, Strawberry Hill, Twickenham, TW1 4SX

PROPHET ELIAS COMMUNITY COLLEGE, PO Box 102, Ibillin 30012, Galilee. Israel Tel: 972-4-9866848. Fax: 972-4-986957_3

SABEEL LIBERATION THEOLOGY CENTRE. PO Box 1248, Jerusalem. Tel: 972-2-289415. Fax: 972-2-283869. E-mail: sabeel@plant.edu

ST GEORGE's CATHEDRAL, St George's Cathedral Close, PO Box 19018, East Jerusalem 91190. via Israel. Tel: 972-2-283261. Fax: 972-2-273401

WORLD VISION. PO Box 51399, An-Nuzha Building, 2 Abu Obeida Street, East Jerusalem. via Israel Tel: 972-2-281793. Fax: 972-2-272065.